D0649889

The Function of Social Work
In a Changing Society:
A Continuum of Practice

By

LOUIS LOWY, Ph.D.

Charles River Books, Inc.
Boston
1976

Library of Congress Cataloging in Publication Data

Lowy, Louis.

The function of social work in a changing society.
Includes bibliographical references.

1. Social service. I. Title.

HV40.L87   361   76-50533

ISBN: 0 89182 004 3

ISBN: 0 89182 005 1 (pb)

Published by Charles River Books, Inc.

59 Commercial Wharf, Boston, Massachusetts 02110

ISBN 0 89182 004 3

ISBN 0 89182 005 1 (pb)

Library of Congress Card Number 76-50533

Printed in The United States of America

CONTENTS

PREFACE

This monograph is the first of two that were requested in 1971 by a number of Swiss social work educators who have been engaged in designing a curriculum for their newly created schools of social work, notably the one in Solothurn under the leadership of Dr. Anton Hunziker and Mr. Joseph Ziltener. Since I have been conducting a series of seminars on social work practice with groups, supervision of social workers, adult educational approaches and methods, curriculum design and development in Germany, Switzerland, France, Belgium and Norway over the past ten years, I have become quite familiar with the problems and issues facing social workers and educators in their own countries. My activities overseas have certainly widened my perspective and sharpened my perceptions of social work that, in turn, have influenced my activities in practice and education in this country to a considerable extent. Recognizing the diversities of social programs and social work practice that are conditioned by different political, economic, social and cultural milieus, I have come to discover firsthand the commonalities and similarities that permeate our field and render it a common base. Yes, there is a unifying thread running through social work that gives it an identity all its own and creates a kinship among its practitioners all over the globe. You have only to attend an international gathering that brings together social workers from the far corners of the earth, to experience a feeling of brotherhood that acknowledges differences in the details of our work, but links us in its essentials.

In these times when the justification for the existence of social work is being questioned again (as it has been so often in the past), I have come to the conclusion that without it many, many people in every country would be significantly deprived of a major instrumentality for human betterment. Or, to apply an old cliché: if social work did not exist, it would have to be created. But since it exists, let us apply our energies towards keeping it continuously relevant to the demands of changing societies, the needs and aspirations of people and towards improving its capabilities of delivering quality services as a partner of social movements and social occupations which are mandated to enhance the conditions of life of all people.

I hope this first monograph will contribute its modest share toward this end and invite comments, promote discussion and stimulate further thoughts across two continents. May it reach particularly those who want to make social work their career and all students who have already embarked on it and are engaged in the process of wrestling with the functions of social work in a fast-changing world.

Spring 1974   L. L.

What is Social Work Today?

Many definitions exist in many countries of the world and many descriptions are offered in documents published by the United Nations (1). But so far no common agreement has been reached by all countries. However, there is consensus that social work is a field of practice and for those who engage in this field it is an occupation. As a field of practice and as an occupation, it has achieved sanction and considerable legitimation in a large number of countries, although there is still a question as to what extent social work is a profession (2). In the United States and Canada the continuing debate of this issue has been temporarily settled in favor of calling it a "semi-profession," placing it on a continuum of vocation-profession and viewing it as being on the road towards increased professionalization (3). The drive towards professionalization is intimately related to the division of labor in modern industrial societies with its attendant specialization, coupled with a desire for an exclusive mandate by the public and a commensurate license that bestows status and prestige upon the occupation (4). Professionalization, however, means more than prerogatives of the professionals. It is also a process by which some, rather than other, occupations become the leading groups from which are drawn the dominating forces in the establishment (5). Small wonder then that occupations seek to become professions; it affects recruitment, training, career development, public confidence and power. The models of the professions of law and medicine are potent attractions: they exert strong pulls upon less traditional callings, and social work has not been immune to these any more than have been nursing, teaching and many other occupations.

It is unlikely that the issue of professional recognition of social work will be settled in the abstract or by academic protestations. It is more likely that it will be resolved if social work can demonstrate to the public of any society that it performs indispensable functions which are in the interest of the public good. Therefore, it is more advantageous at this time to look at social work as a field of practice. As such it is engaged in a series of activities to achieve defined ends. Such activities are functional for society and are carried out by people who are knowledgeable about the activities, their functional relationship and the defined ends. In addition, there must be a mandate by the general public to engage in such activities which is usually manifested in a certain degree of confidence in the people who practice and a willingness to submit to their ministrations. Once the general public underpins such a mandate with legal sanctions and gives practitioners a license with attendant prerogatives and privileges, a field of practice has become a profession. Law and medicine and theology are the most notable illustrations of this phenomenon. As yet, social work in no country of the world has achieved such a status (6).

There is a more analytic way to define a field of practice. We can delineate it in terms of its major components that make up its endeavors: 1) a set of values to which it adheres and to which it shows varying degrees of commitment; 2) the goals or purposes toward which it is directed and for which ends it carries out its activities; 3) sanctions that give it legitimacy in the eyes of the public and which support the auspices under which it operates; 4) a knowledge base which underlies its activities; and 5) a methodology or an interventive repertoire which it deploys to translate knowledge into skillful action (7).

Though each of these five components can be analyzed separately, it is the combination of all these parts that produces the particular characteristics of a field of practice or an occupation. Social work is no exception. In the United States a great deal of effort has been devoted to analyze the practice of social work according to these components and further attempts along these lines are going on presently (8).

The constellation of the five components must be placed in a societal context since no practice operates in a vacuum. It is the matrix of a given society which shapes the value base and the goals and purposes, which provides sanctions and auspice and which influences the knowledge base and the type of methodology that a field employs. A society which concentrates on the use of technical methods in the solution of human problems will develop different social practices from a society which gives priority to non-technical methods. Social work is embedded in the matrix of a societal milieu.

2

The Societal Matrix of Social Work

The societal matrix of social work is the environment which gives rise to its very existence. All fields of human endeavors have been and continue to be a response to an environment and also proceed to have an effect upon the environment. A particular environment gives rise also to a particular response; what constitutes a particular environment, i.e. the delineation of its parameters, becomes crucial in order to place social work within a societal context.

The Judaeo-Christian religions have held that man is apart from nature: nature is created for man's use. The consequences of such a view have led to a rather intensive and extensive exploitation of man's eco-system with little regard for man's immediate environment, as evidenced in our belated recognition of environmental pollution. When man is seen as part of nature the conditions of the eco-system are included in man's conception of the environment with concomitant consequences for the potentiality of action.

Accepting this latter view, human conduct and interaction occur in an arena that is characterized by four major phenomena: 1) space 2) time 3) matter and 4) people. Territory, time, material resources and population are phenomena which influence and shape the manifestations of nature in their myriad ways: the latter are in turn influenced and shaped by these phenomena. This reciprocal interplay is a major truth which has become universally accepted in the scientific community. The precise extent and the exact proportion of this interplay has been, is and will be at the heart of scientific inquiry of yesterday, today and tomorrow. The way man adjusts, reacts and attempts to bend that which exists to his desires and designs is the saga of man. How he struggles and copes with space on this earth (and now even beyond), with topography and geography, with matter material and energy and thereby creates a technology, how he behaves vis à vis his fellowmen and vis à vis himself, how he relates to events in the past and how he attempts to

3

continue his existence and his non-existence, all these constitute the human drama, its tragedy and its comedy chronicled by historians, investigated by scientists, narrated by poets, dramatists and novelists, and portrayed in pictures or in stone by artists.

Territory, material resources, and population through time give rise to and influence man's culture that essentially "is a system of beliefs, values and expressive symbols which govern man's relations to his fellowmen and to his (physical) environment" (9). Culture has several segments. A social structure or a social order is one such segment; it comes into being through a set of ideas that define rights and obligations comprising the positions which people occupy in groups. Technology is another segment; it represents the application of knowledge of nature to empirical ends, i.e. ends which are attainable by man. Technology, therefore, is always instrumental to a goal and goals are influenced, if not shaped, by beliefs and values that have emerged through time. Nature is the environment which is both: physical and cultural.

All social life arises from man's attempts to respond to the demands of the physical and cultural environment and to solve the problems which are posed to his existence and survival and which he shares with other men everywhere throughout all times. His elemental drive to survive in a physical and cultural milieu on the one hand, and his desire to find a purpose and meaning for this survival on the other, have led to a series of attempts to devise solutions which are time-and-place-specific and circumscribed by culture. When these attempts have occurred in a seemingly sequential order, they are referred to as "history".

Students of society throughout history have identified a series of problems which have to be solved in order to assure a continued existence of culture, of society and of man himself. From this vantage point society's existential concerns for survival prescribe certain solutions which will assure its ability to cope with environmental or natural forces and to perpetuate its existence. Whether these solutions are also in the best interest of man is a different question, since man himself is an entity and part of nature. His drives for survival as a human being are existential to him as are his desires for deriving meaning and purpose of his being. These drives and desires get expressed as human needs, although the way in which they are individually expressed and manifested depends on the time and place

4

and cultural specificity of the milieu. This is what is meant by man's social nature. At times man's needs are more congruent with those of his society of which he is a part; at other times they are less congruent, at variance and their resulting tensions are of major concern in any society. Mankind's history is an account of the way in which societies have expressed this concern, how they have handled it, and what mechanisms they have developed to deal with inevitable tensions. Changing beliefs, (including religious ones), values and ideologies have played a major role in this development. Those societies that have moved toward greater recognition of this concern and have actively sought out mechanisms to manage arising tensions, not only for "the good of society" but also for the "good of human beings," have usually created structural arrangements to manage these tensions. These societies have addressed themselves to human and social welfare, since human and social welfare is not necessarily synonymous with societal welfare, notwithstanding many statements to the contrary in capitalistic and socialistic countries.

Basic Features of Societies: A Series of Functions

As was mentioned, every society has to solve a series of problems to exist and to survive in a physical and cultural environment. In order to do so it must perform a series of functions. How it solves these universal problems and how it performs these requisite functions is at the same time conditioned by the physical and cultural environment and by the passage of time, by history and by traditions. Five major functions can be enumerated: 1) Provisions for the Population 2) Allocation of Resources and Property Rights 3) Maintenance of Order With Justice 4) Assurance of Continuity and Socialization 5) Creation of Social Intergration Through Participation (10).

1) Provisions for the Population:

Every society must assure the physical survival of its people through provision of food, clothing and shelter (housing). How it manages this function varies widely and is influenced by major physical and cultural variables, not in the least by its religious, ideological or value commitments. For the individual human being, his drive to exist demands that his need for food, clothing and shelter be satisfied every hour of his life, although the way in which he expects satisfaction is influenced by major physical and cultural variables such as climate, geography, technology, beliefs, etc.

In most countries there is recognition now that minimum provision to insure physical survival of its people is an obligation of society. There is still widespread disagreement as to what forms such an obligation should take. In practically all societies the means to insure human physical survival in the form of income are linked with a demand that they perform work to get the necessary tasks of society done. To put it another way, income and work are viewed as reciprocal and the ancient dictum that "only those who work shall eat" is by no means obsolete today, as is the Old Testament

6

injunction of having "to earn your bread by the sweat of your brow". To be sure, many societies exempt large segments from the population from certain work requirements, e.g. the very young, the very old, the sick and the infirm and provide for their food, clothing and shelter. If there is not enough work to go around, (unemployment), societies make attempts to assure some modicum of these provisions as well. In order to do so various mechanisms have been developed over time which reflect various technological and cultural changes in a particular society.

However, the general provision of food, clothing and shelter through income has largely been left to the interplay of the forces of supply and demand in capitalistic economies and to the forces of economic planning by the government in socialistic countries. In special circumstances this provision is either assumed by special social welfare institutions based on an insurance principle to effect a more equitable distribution of the social product, or handled residually under the rubric of charity. Recently the idea of a guaranteed income, regardless of ability to work, has taken hold in some countries. It presents a new advance in man's thinking, since it divorces the reciprocity of work and income and establishes the principle of man's right to income regardless of his ability or desire to work, based on a view of man as a "being man" rather than as a "doing man". This view has received impetus under the impact of technological advances which has resulted in an increased leisure made possible for larger segments of a population (11).

Social welfare institutions in society which are charged with provisional functions mentioned above are designed to provide social insurance programs, social assistance or public assistance programs, unemployment and workmen's compensation, etc. Essentially, they are income maintenance or income subsistence provisions mostly under public auspices, although the private sector in capitalistic countries participates through a number of pension schemes which supplement the public programs. These "social security" measures are the results of a society's social policy that had its beginnings in the second half of the nineteenth century in a few Western European countries, notably in Germany and Great Britain. Since that time more and more countries all over the world have adopted a distinctive social policy (as distinguished from an undifferentiated domestic policy). Today a

7

social policy with attendant financial and social programs and services to assure minimal existential security, if not yet comprehensive social security, is considered an inherent part of any society, although the type, scope, benefits, organization, etc. of such existing programs vary considerably from country to country (12). As of 1973 in one hundred and twenty-nine countries at least some type of social security program was available protecting their people from such risk conditions as old age invalidity, death of breadwinner, sickness, work injury, or unemployment (12 a).

Not only food, clothing and shelter, which are largely obtainable through income, must be assured if a society wants its population to exist. How its population can be kept in tact. how disease and injuries to the people can be prevented and death delayed, how a modicum balance of healthy people can be maintained is another major task that must be tackled. This means that every society must find solutions to the problems of ill-health of a physical, mental and emotional nature, and to strive towards its cure and prevention. Expressed positively it means that societies must find ways and means to promote good health among its people (13). Mechanisms to cope with these concerns have to be created and in all societies institutions have been developed to deal with problems of ill-health. Variations abound in the approach to health care, the care of the sick and the infirm, and the prevention of disease and the maintenance of good health; all these are affected by differing technologies and by uneven access to material and human resources. There is a proven correlation between a society's wealth and the state of health of its population.

Not only are societies concerned about the health of their people: individuals themselves strive to remain in good health, since they want to experience a state of physical, mental and emotional well-being. In an increasingly larger number of societies this need has come to be more and more accepted as much of a right as the entitlement to food, shelter and clothing (14). Individuals want to be able to take part in the affairs of daily living in as healthy a state as possible; in an age of rising expectations they want to have access to all the provisions of good health care which modern science has made possible. Although there seems to be some degree of congruence between societal and individual needs, there are inevitable discrepancies between them as there are also in the area of income provisions. There are discrepancies between the way individuals perceive their needs and wants and the way society perceives its imperatives and obligations. There are discrepancies between the way individuals think and feel their health needs should be met and society's willingness and ability to do so. There are discrepancies between the access an individual has to diagnosis and treatment facilities and society's concern for access to health facilities for the masses to assure large–scale coverage of needs. Here, as everywhere, there are built–in tensions between the needs of individual people and the needs of an abstract society; provisions which a society deems essential to assure its existential survival—even when it espouses the doctrine that it is for the good of the people—are not ipso facto sufficient to satisfy the wants, desires and aspirations of human beings as individuals, as members of families or other groups, as members of neighborhoods in communities. These built–in tensions need mechanisms for resolution; they need mediating devices.

Besides assuring food, clothing and shelter and a modicum of good health to its people, the patterning of sex relations to ensure motivation and opportunity for a sufficient rate of reproduction strikes at the core of any societal function. Small wonder that every society has created mores and taboos, rules and norms that govern this aspect of life and death of a social order. Because the sex drives (as hunger drives) are probably the most pervasive drives of men, societies are anything but indifferent towards how sex drives are channelled, and they make sure that they accrue to their maximum advantage. Consequently, the tensions that exist between the needs of individuals for sexual gratification and the demands of society for an orderly process of sexual activity which is beneficial to society require mediating efforts and arrangements. The institution of the family has assumed major regulation functions in this arena, although changing values, mores and functions have given rise nowadays to new and different tensions which the family as an institution cannot easily handle. The family, however, is more than an instrument for procreation. It additionally fulfills economic, educational, religious social-psychological functions for its members, although changing cultural conditions in industrialized societies have divested the family of some of these functions and turned them over to other social institutions (15). As a result, family life itself has undergone an upheaval frought with stress, and many individuals' needs, particularly

9

the affective, emotional ones, are frequently not met. For a number of people traditional family life itself has become a source of major stress; they seek other types of living arrangements, such as communes, or turn to other social institutions for relief.

The built-in conflict between man's needs and societal "needs" is evident and is "normal". This has been man's history on this earth since man has created social organization to make life manageable. With increasing complexities of life in a post-industrialized society*, with proliferation of institutions and proliferation of people, with cultural changes at an accelerated pace that offer man unprecedented opportunities for existential fulfillment on this earth, but that also have opened up the specter of man's annihilation, man will and must assert his needs vis à vis those of society and look for a mediating mechanism; such a mechanism is social work since its major goal is to mediate between problems of the individual and his (her) family as (a) member(s) of society and problems of society, manifested in social institutions, as they affect the individual.

2) Allocation of Resources and Property Rights:

Every society faces the problem of allocation of its material, financial, spatial and human resources. Until recent times, all societies had to contend with the scarcity of all of these resources and to cut their cloths accordingly. Through advances in and mobilization of technology many, if not most, industrialized societies have been able to create an abundance of material goods and certain types of services. In many instances private wants have superseded public needs (16). However, even those countries that have been able to "lick" problems of production have faced difficulties in handling problems of distribution and consumption. The United States is a good illustration. But most of all everywhere in the world

---

*Post-industrialized society is characterized by reliance on computer technology, increased material well being of larger segments of the population, increased social interdependence, rapid technological changes with concomitant speed of obsolesence, by mass communication media and by emergence of large-scale bureaucratic organizations.

there are severe shortages in human resources, especially in the availability of skilled brain and muscle power, despite the fact that in some countries greater educational opportunities have been able to create more such manpower. To find appropriate solutions to produce and distribute, as equitably as possible, the various resources of a society has become a major issue of this century and has linked economic concerns with concerns for social justice. The shrinkage of spatial distances between countries has opened up new vistas for resource exchange, although spatial proximity alone is not likely to produce an economically better balanced world. In fact, the poorer countries of the globe have become poorer at the same time that the richer nations have become richer (17). Obviously the issues of maldistribution of resources is tied up with political and economic power plays.

In addition to dealing with allocation of resources every society has to grapple with allocation of property rights on an individual, group, community and nation-state level in order to assure the flow of production and distributions of goods and services to carry out transactions in the agricultural, commercial, industrial and service sectors. Division of labor is a hallmark of industrialization. Control of property and the right to possess and dispose of it has been a major issue throughout man's history, but has indeed become a major source of conflict since the beginning of the industrial revolution. This conflict, intimately connected with issues of social justice and allocation of resources, permeates the struggles of our days on a world-wide scale. The question of whether human rights or property rights have priority on the scale of values of a society has by no means been settled in favor of human rights in most societies, despite professions to the contrary. The evidence for this can be found in judicial decisions, in tax laws, and in national budgetary allocations.

Specialized tasks to carry out economic functions require a source of specially trained people. Educational institutions in post-industrialized societies particularly had to adapt to these demands and to cease being meeting grounds for an elite. Education became training-oriented to "produce" workers and thinkers to man the production lines, the distribution centers and the consumption-promotion agencies of a goods and services industry. Educational functions and training functions have merged considerably today and are often indistinguishable.

11

The economic needs of people are frequently out of tune with the needs of society for smooth economic functioning. Personal wants and desires in the economic sphere often outstrip the allocations which society makes for the satisfaction of these desires—even in planned societies—since economic planning even under the best of circumstances cannot meet individualized needs in every respect and on every level. Economic security and allocation of resources are closely related. Among individuals the world over there is increasing expectation that society should manage its affairs in such a way that appropriate production and distribution of goods and services make individual economic security possible. Or expressed in another way: there are rising expectations that absolute economic poverty will be eliminated through better management of resources and re-assessment of property rights and that greater economic equalization will assure a minimum income floor for everybody. The discrepancy between needs of people to partake of resources and to be in control of their destiny, and societal prerequisites to manage and control resources and to effect property rights—even for "the good of the people"— produces tensions that call for mediation and amelioration. While an enlightened economic and social policy can move towards a more egalitarian social democracy, many individuals and families will continue to face problems in the economic sector that call for interventive mechanisms some of which social work can provide through assistance in financial management capabilities of people in various economic circumstances.

Besides, many people do not find the demands of particular occupations commensurate with their own desires and aspirations. Such incompatibility evokes stress leading to frustration, unhappiness and apathy. From a societal perspective, certain jobs have to be done and it is to society's interest that they be done well. Unhappy people are not good at doing jobs well. Reconciliation of such incompatibility calls for interventive efforts.

3) Maintenance of Order with Justice:

Another function of a social system is to protect its people from within and from without against the use of violence, and to forestall a war of all against all. Such protection has to be extended to all its members equally. The history of mankind is filled with pages of bloody encounters, of unequal treatment, of offenders and offended, and of order without justice. Since the relations of people with one another are of fundamental concern to every society (it touches on its very existence), it is small wonder that the development of commandments and rules and their codifications into laws and ordinances have been a major task of social systems. Mechanisms to assure adherence to such laws and ordinances have resulted in sanctions for violations (also in rewards for conformity) and these, in turn, have produced political, legal, and correctional institutions, e.g. governments, courts, police, armies, prisons, etc. The creation of authority positions among the population have led to differential distributions of power relations in a given society.

The struggle for power ascendency of individuals and groups within and between societies is another leaf in the pages of man's history. In the name of law and order many a group of people have been subjugated and many crimes have been committed. At the same time the creation of just laws and the administration of justice based on such laws has been the bulwark of a civilized society that assures the rights of people to live in peace and to adjudicate conflicts in a rational and reasonable manner. It makes it possible for people to settle their conflicts without resorting to violence and annihilation. Yet this principle applies so far only to conflicts within a given society. Man has not been able to carry out this principle on an international scale. Despite century-old attempts to introduce an enforceable machinery into international law, relations between countries are still governed by the "law of the jungle". Never has mankind been more vulnerable to this threat of annihilation as today; technology has not only created more opportunities for affluence and human fulfillment, it has also created more opportunities for misery and human destruction.

Power is a fact of social intercourse and social organization. To assure that it is used rather than abused there must be provisions for its observability and accountability. The exercise of power demands control mechanisms because it can inflict harm on people and lead to despotism. In a democratic society such mechanisms must perform the functions of checking and balancing to offset a preponderance and massing of power in one center of society; holders of positions of authority must be answerable and accountable to the people; the stewardship in their positions must be observable to the people and opportunities must be provided for the change of the incumbents to avoid entrenchment and the vesting of interests to the detriment of the rest of the population.

Individuals have a need to be in control of their own destiny and to be autonomous. The growth from infancy to mature adulthood is essentially a process of becoming gradually more and more autonomous within a context of a tribe or a family and peers. Individuals also need to be protected from willful, capricious acts by others, whether in positions of authority or not; they want to be protected from acts of violence, both physical and non-physical, and from being exploited by others. Obviously these needs, like all others, are reciprocal and therefore the balance between people's needs and societal imperatives is as tenuous here as in all other aspects of life. For this reason continuous attention, alertness, vigilance and mediation are called for to assure order with justice—and to protect people against the very protection of those who place the interest of societal survival (not social survival) above the interest of human survival. The roles of social work in this arena are by no means insignificant as a broker and advocate.

4) Assurance of Continuity and Socialization:

Infants are born helpless everywhere. Therefore some provisions have to be made for infant and child care, for the socialization of the young to the culture of a society and for the continuity of the culture into the future. To carry out these functions a society develops mechanisms for communication, for child-rearing and socialization and for re-socialization of those who deviate from the social and cultural norms. In the Western world these mechanisms include the family, educational and religious institutions and the social welfare system in its broadest sense of the term. In the recent past much overlap between these institutional functions has occurred and domain disputes have arisen. Many of these institutions have undergone functional and structural changes and have been challenged in rapidly changing societies as to their adequacy and relevance. In some instances new responses have been forthcoming and adaptations to new demands have resulted in better performances of their tasks; this has been true of some educational institutions, religious bodies and social welfare agencies in North America and in several countries of Western and Eastern Europe. It is too early yet to say whether new institutions will emerge or whether the old ones are flexible

14

enough to adapt sufficiently to assure continuity. The fact remains that the "crisis of institutions" is in itself a significant phenomenon today and unsettles man as an individual as much as it unsettles society itself.

It has been assumed that man needs to learn in order to master the environment as well as to actualize himself as a human being. Although there is complementarity between societal imperatives to perpetuate the social system and the culture through socialization of the members, and man's desires to acquire knowledge and to be part of the culture, there are considerable tensions between the press of the social system and the wishes of the people to pursue their own bend and their own interests as far as knowledge acquisition is concerned, to grow and develop at their own pace and even to deviate from established norms. In performing child-rearing, socialization and re-socialization functions the various social institutions are oriented to assure the continuity of the culture and also the good and welfare of these institutions; however the good and welfare of human beings—for whom presumably these institutions have been created—warrant attention, and their desires for learning, mastery, growth and development as human beings need to be emphasized as the conflict between their goals and those of the social institutions needs mediation. Social work has such a mediating function.

5) Creation of Social Integration:

No society can hold together unless its people are sufficiently motivated to, at least, tolerate one another, to resist outside intruders, to plan their conduct to fit in roughly with what others expect. This condition is usually referred to as cohesiveness, solidarity or social integration. People must want to belong to a society, to a culture; they must want to work together, to be together, to participate in the affairs of a society. Solidarity is promoted through a variety of mechanisms such as ideology and symbols, through display of charisma, through rewards or punishments. Recently a democratic ethos that emphasizes participation of members in society as much as maximally feasible has led to several new modes of social decision-making in a number of institutions in the United States and to a new consciousness as to the rights and responsibilities of consumers, clients, patients, students, ethnic and racial groups in the conduct of social and educational programs and services. (18). Many social institutions promote solidarity and foster bonds among people. The family, religion, social welfare, education, to name the major ones, are oriented to foster social participation and mutual aid. In the recent past the tenets of social participation, born in the political philosophies of the 18th century and buttressed in the social philosophies of the 19th and 20th centuries, have found fertile ground in the political, social and economic realities of many societies as they have developed since World War II, such as in Europe, North and Latin America, and in many parts of Asia and Africa.

That man is altruistic by nature is by no means established; however, man's gregariousness is quite well accepted by psychologists the world over. His gregarious nature makes him a *"zoon politikon"*, a social being, and thereby creates conditions for his social participation in the affairs of a society. Apparently man can tolerate others, can move toward acceptance of others, can collaborate with others, can share with others and can bestow love on others. In turn, man needs to be tolerated, to be accepted, to be worked with, to be loved. Viewed negatively, man can be intolerant of other men, can reject others, can dominate and subjugate others, can work against other men and can dislike and hate others. The Jekyll and Hyde nature of man is his personal drama and makes up man's personality. Nature and nurture make life and living possible, and allow for the interplay between man and his society. Man's relations with his fellow-men, for good or evil, are at the roots of this interplay. We have now reached a stage in the affairs of man when mutual toleration, if not acceptance, becomes a prime condition for man's survival on this earth. Integration and solidarity are no longer confined to a particular culture or society; they have become of concern to all mankind transcending the concept of a particular society and extending it to encompass all nations.

Because of man's apparent contradictory nature and the difficulties encountered in his relationship to other people as individuals or members of groups or even societies, mediating efforts are again called for to negotiate the tensions and conflicts, to make it possible for man to gratify his desires and his needs for love and affection, to be himself, to achieve his identity as a person, to fulfill himself in relation with others as a psychosocial being, to face and to handle those tasks that are incumbent upon himself as he goes through life from birth to death as a social participant. Social

16

work as a field concerned with human and social relations towards social integration has a function in this arena.

All functions that must be performed by a society (and that have been enumerated so far) lead to allocation of status and roles, to their differentiation and hence to social stratification. People classify each other and are classified in turn on a scale of "superiority and inferiority" (19). Distinctions are made as some people are given greater authority over others, power and prestige differentiations appear. Man has made such differentiations according to color, class, religion, nationality and has created a series of distinctions based on income, property, creed, color, ideology, background and a host of others. Depending on the hierarchy of values that exists in a given society some distinctive groups and positions are honored, others are not, because a society bestows prestige upon those groups, positions, and roles that approximate closest its highest values. For instance in the USA industrial and professional entrepreneurs, and in the USSR political commissars and highly productive workers, are on the top of the prestige ladder; in industrialized, developed societies the young are preferred over the old who still hold many prerogatives in agricultural and traditional societies. Social inequalities and commensurate stratifications have been the root of social unrest throughout the ages. Despite the *zeitgeist* of today, which abstractly rejects privilege and special prerogatives, inequalities in societies do persist. They prevail even though the value-bases tend to shift in a number of societies, notably, but not exclusively the socialist countries, and attempts are made to base differentiations on competence rather than on status, on role performance rather than on role ascription, on acquired authority, rather than on inherited authority, on the principle of greater inclusiveness superiority. Nevertheless, the process of shifting is slow, uneven within and among societies and creates severe stresses and strains in today's world. Many individuals are subjected to these stresses and strains and need interventive assistance to cope. Social work can provide such assistance.

There are two major forces which affect the way in which societies go about solving their functional problems: 1) technology and 2) beliefs, ideas and values.

Several sociologists have held to a technological determinism (20) stating that the basic causes of social change can be found in

17

the changes over time in technology. Undoubtedly, technology has played an enormous role in our social history and we can all agree that technology as an instrumental segment of culture has been most influential in giving rise to a post-industrial society in many parts of the world. We have seen that technology has affected and does affect the social institutions that have arisen as a response to solving the various societal functions which have been discussed. The various cultural, social and economic institutions have been affected by the technological advances since the invention of the steam engine, the harnessing of electricity, the use of nuclear power. Yet for technology to be that powerful there must be a commitment to certain beliefs and values which support the preeminence of technology and its attendant influence upon human affairs. Such values would include a belief in economic progress, conquest of "nature" by man, extension of the life span of man, etc. Perhaps it is more appropriate to ascribe a prime moving force to values and beliefs which have a powerful influence upon the way a society defines its functional problems, how it orders them, what it considers vital and important, what counts most and what counts least. For this reason it is imperative to understand the order of priority of values, beliefs and ideas and to analyze the value orientation and perspective of a given society.

Does a society view its functional problems from a status-quo, equilibrium and harmony perspective or does it view them from a changing, disequilibrium and conflict perspective? The former essentially holds that society seeks an equilibrium of its many groups as a natural boundary which strives to maintain a balanced system of action, and that the functional problems must be solved by strengthening and, when needed, improving its social institutions which are basically intact. The latter views society as a contested struggle between myriad, heterogeneous groups and the functional problems as requiring new solutions and new approaches that may not result in permanent social institutions, but in ad hoc "institutions" ready to be abandoned when they are no longer responsive to ever changing demands. Obviously both perspectives are ideal-type extremes and serve only as "models" to place various approaches in bolder relief (21). In the "order or equilibrium perspective" a society will place great emphasis upon maintaining law and order to assure socialization and continuity, while in the "conflict or disequilibrium perspective" the emphasis will be more on

18

justice towards different groups of people, to assure their personal fulfillment as human beings and their continuity, and thereby to justify the continued existence of a social structure. Stated in the extreme, this latter perspective holds that the survival of man in his humaneness is more important than the survival of society. Whether such a dichotomy can occur in practice is of course highly questionable.

Man's Needs and Society's Imperatives

Throughout this discourse we have stated a dichotomous condition which is inherent in the existence of man and of society: society must solve certain problems to insure its continued existence, and to fulfill its "needs" or imperatives, and man must solve certain problems to insure his continued existence within a social matrix and to fulfill his needs and aspirations which frequently are not in harmony with those of his society. Man's symbiotic interdependent relationship with his society and his variance of needs from those of his society produce a series of tensions accompanied by stresses and strains. Maslow has constructed a needs-system for man that postulates a hierarchy of needs. He points out that the higher types of human needs can be gratified only after the lower types have been gratified first. He places at the bottom the physiological and safety needs and then moves upwards to the needs for love and belonging, to those for esteem, achievement and recognition, to self-actualization and finally to the needs to "know and understand" (22). We encounter with him a number of needs which correspond, in some measure, to societal imperatives, although no theoretical hierarchical system has been developed for those as has been done by Maslow for human needs.

It is precisely the unevenness of "fit" between the needs of a society and the needs of its individual members that result in tensions which demand attention. The social milieu makes a number of demands on its people that are often at odds with their desires and needs. At various stages of life there are particular demands made upon people which have to be met by them. These have been referred to as developmental tasks occurring during a person's lifetime, in infancy, childhood, adolescence, young adulthood, in the middle and later years and in old age (23). There is always a certain degree of disequilibrium between societal demands and a person's ability to cope with them despite "training" for them during a socialization process. Some people manage better than others; they are then referred to as "functioning better socially". In times of accelerated, rapid social change (cultural, technical and social) tensions usually increase and generally people find it harder to cope than during times of greater stability and tranquility.

But coping with varying and complicated demands at a particular stage in the life cycle are not the only concerns of man. He has a variety of needs that may not be fulfilled in the way he wants them fulfilled and at a time when he is ready for them. He may reasonably well have met his physiological, safety and esteem needs; he is now ready to seek gratification for his higher needs, winning from life a sense of purpose and meaning, actualizing himself and understanding the world and his own existence in it. He is now ready to take part in enjoying the gifts of life and nature, to enhance the quality of his own living, of his family, peers and friends; he is now ready to engage responsibly and creatively to improve the lives of others in his Faustian endeavors. We are therefore not only concerned with man's "social functioning" but also with man's "existential fulfillment" as a social participant, *"Realisierung der sozialen und politischen Dimensionen des Mensch Seins"* (24). Man today must be able to actualize himself not only as a member of *his* culture, *his* society, but also learn to do so as a member of world society and the culture of all men. Admittedly this is still presently a vision, but a desirable and a necessary one. To strive towards its achievement tomorrow is worthy of our best efforts today.

To assure man a minimum floor for his existence, i.e. social security, to make him capable of "social functioning" to the best of his ability as well as to make him capable of "existential fulfillment" as a social participant in the world of tomorrow, requires a number of social mechanisms and arrangements.

Social Mechanisms to Create Social Security and Existential Fulfillment

Two major mechanisms are available to a society to develop social security for its population, i.e., a system designed to assure optimal existential conditions of people: social policies and social practices. These two mechanisms can be used to make people capable of "social functioning" and also to make them realize their maximum potential, to achieve existential fulfillment as social participants. This existential fulfillment goes beyond the level of experiencing a secure economic existence, even under the best of circumstances; it is the opportunity to experience maximum human growth as a participating member of society which is predicated upon assured economic and social security. To put it another way, social security is the floor upon which the ladder towards personal and social fulfillment of people can be erected.

Both mechanisms, social policies and social practices, are interventive in nature and are "of society". Both are concerned with social functioning of man as well as with his fulfillment as a human social being. Social policies are "interventions and regulations of an otherwise random social system" (25) and operate on a macro-level. They are designed to "promote the welfare of the whole population through a system of laws, programs and services" (26). In Schorr's words a social policy is a "course of action with respect to selected social phenomena governing social relationships and the distribution of resources within a society" (27). As such it functions as a societal institution primarily concerned with social provisions for the population. Social insurances, health insurances, unemployment programs, care for the sick and the disabled, etc., are manifestations and features of a social policy. In several countries there has been a broadening of this conception to extend across the range of governmentally and nongovernmentally provided social and health services and all governmental intervention in the private market (28). Increasingly all

22

economic policy is seen as part of social policy and distribution of income and resources is viewed as germaine to social policy (29).

Within this context social policy is designed to build a social security system for the total population. The extent of a society's social policy and its resulting laws, programs and services is conditioned by the social philosophy, value commitment, history, tradition and a host of other variables. Recently a number of social policy makers in a number of countries have expressed interest in the goals of human fulfillment and in the inclusion of educational policy as part of social policy (30). Domain autonomy and system boundary maintenance, however, are still powerful enough to thwart such inclusive efforts at the present time. At any rate, social policies have increasingly come to be seen as pillars of "social security" (31) in Western and Eastern Europe, if not yet in the USA where there does not yet exist "a clearly comprehensive statement of national goals or a social policy encompassing such goals" (32).

Social Policy and Societal Policy

The tasks of social policy in many dynamic societies go beyond the present ones. Studer, for example, calls for research and planning of social structures and social behavior, constructive influence attempt upon socialization and acculturation measures to enable people to shape their environment (33). In other words, social policy should become societal policy which influences the various societal functions already discussed, in order to create conditions for man to find creative fulfillment and self-realization as a social participant. Thus, societal policy would indeed become the frame of reference which guarantees man not only existential social security but also enables him to achieve existential fulfillment.

Societal policy of the future will be based on empirical research, social prognosis and social planning, and will require projection of a social future which can be extrapolated from the present (34).

The goals of such societal policy should be primarily directed towards changing the structures (e.g. social institutions) to make them more responsive to changing human needs within a societal context, and toward changing socio-cultural values and norms that are inimical to a healthy growth and development of people and therefore inhibit their full-range existential fulfillment through social participation.

Such goals can be achieved through appropriate and knowledgeable use of social interventive or planning methods, which are predicated upon a problem-solving approach. "This mode of intervention in social problems rests on the assumption that their causes lie not in individual dysfunction but in system dysfunction and the inability of the community to provide the basic necessities of food, clothing, shelter; protection against disease, disaster and war; requisite social necessities of social power distribution, social communication, social control, and common value systems" (35).

"Social-problem solving originates in a recognition on the part of an individual or a group that there is a disjunction between an existing social situation (e.g. higher rates of infant mortality or youth employment among minority groups) and an ideal state or standard (the elimination of differences in such rates that are attributable to race or ethnicity). The recognition of a gap between present reality and some valued future state provides the impetus for initiating activities that are managed by an individual or group who have been mandated or who have assumed the responsibility for planning" (36).

The main constellation of activities (also frequently referred to as "methods of social planning") is the following: describing and analyzing the problematic conditions and identification of possible explanations for its existence; probing the preferences and influence of persons who are presumably relevant to the problem at hand; obtaining commitments to the desired changes; designing and implementing a monitoring system of feedback, which in turn generates new tasks for planning. These activities are not carried out in a simple sequence. Each is pursued repeatedly in interacting spiral-like patterns. Essentially two sets of activities have to be performed by the social planner: analytic and interactional tasks. On the one hand he has to analyze the "facts", the problem conditions, the politics of contending interests and influence; on the other hand he has to engage in interorganizational, intergroup and interpersonal communication and in the development of relationships with people (37).

In short, societal policy in the future, in its concern with social system functioning, will have to be planning-oriented in order to ensure societal provisions for a country's total population so that a social, economic and cultural standard can be met which is commensurate with the prevailing social, economic and cultural advances in that particular society, and which are ultimately available in other societies throughout the world.

As we have seen, there are always tensions between what a society can and will provide, even under the best of circumstances, and what man needs and wants because of nature and of nurture.

The very institutions that man has created follow their "laws of functional autonomy" (38), (they evolve an existence of their own), and due to sheer size and complexity cannot be responsive to man's needs at all times, or even most of the time. The inherent strains between the demands of man's inner self and social roles and tasks at any stage of a person's life call for resolution. Some people can cope better with such demands than others and some do worse than others. Societies have made some provisions for such events and instances; they have created services, programs and occupations in the health and social sectors. People who have problems with the functioning of their body or in coping with certain life demands can see a physician, a psychiatrist, a nurse, a social worker, at least in theory. In practice, however, there are often many obstacles between the availability of a service and its accessibility to a potential patient or client. Because of increasing interrelationships between health and intra- and interpersonal problems it is more and more difficult to separate these two, although occupational autonomy is a strong force in keeping quite apart health practitioners and social workers. Today in the USA there is a tendency to speak of "human service" fields and occupations and to seek as much as possible linkages between different types of services. What the eventual name designations of these fields will be is hard to predict.

The field of practice which has carved out for itself a domain in dealing with problems encountered by people with regard to their "social functioning" is social work. It has begun to move beyond a concern for mere "social functioning" toward a striving for human fulfillment and self-realization through active social participation. Social work is a social practice mechanism that intervenes in order to mediate tensions between society's imperatives and man's needs, desires, expectations and aspirations. If societal policy is "of society" then social work is "of people", to use an oversimplified, abstract dichotomy; and yet social work is also "for society" and societal policy is also "for people". Nevertheless, these analytic distinctions may be useful for clarifying the specific emphasis placed on each.

26

The Social Work Practice Continuum

Until recent times the central goal of social work in the United States has been to enable people to improve their social functioning, i.e. to carry out their social roles consistent with their ego capacity, (39) with a major focus on socially assisting (planfully helping) people to cope with life situations and/or conditions which present difficulties. Bartlett has taken this central idea and has elaborated on it by stating that social work attempts to strike a balance between the demands of the social environment and people's coping efforts through directly working with them individually, in small groups or in social organizations or through collaborative action (40). Its primary concern has been and is with people in difficult life situations and in social roles which they find troublesome or difficult to manage. "Treatment" has been a key aspect of this type of social work, despite the fact that American social work has also a long-standing tradition of social reform efforts which have concentrated on "macro-system intervention" to make social institutions more responsive to the needs of people rather than expect people to adhere to and conform to unresponsive social systems. This type of intervention has moved closer to social policy, and now even to societal policy, and there is agreement in the US and elsewhere that a link between these two major modes of intervention is essential (41).

Treatment of people and societal intervention have come to be recognized as only one side of a coin, as one aspect of a continuum. Treatment of disturbed relationships among people, aid in the procurement of financial aid through supplementary income, support during periods of crisis and stress belong to the segment of ameliorative services on the malfunctioning end of the "social-functioning– human-fulfillment" continuum. But people have normal problems of living as well. To meet the daily tasks of human existence in increasingly complex societies, to face up to the demands of being a child in school, or a worker in a factory, to face up to retirement in the later

27

years, or to death in old age, all these "normal" events can become "normal" crises under a certain confluence of variables.

At the other end of the continuum are the functions of growth and development and the enhancement of personal fulfillment; being part of the world in a creative way, being active in improving the human and social conditions for self and others, continuing to learn in order to know and understand oneself and one's fellow human beings, realizing one's own potential and realizing the potential of others. From a person's malfunctioning we move via "normal" functioning to eu-functioning (or optimal functioning), and from amelioration of troublesome conditions and their treatment we move through deliberate, change-oriented action toward development and enhancement of the person in his social world.

The following framework is used to delineate analytically social work as a field of practice on a continuum, set within the societal matrix developed.

Components of Practice

Five components of social work practice will be discussed: Values, Purpose, Sanctions, Knowledge and Intervention Repertoire (42).

Values: All practice is guided by values which are preferred stances of behavior. It may be more appropriate to speak of "valuations" rather than "values", since these imply an immutable universality that is based on "an objectivism that has no basis in logic and tends to conceal much confusion" (43). Valuations are subjective reactions to the property of the "real values", always changing in accordance with changing cultural environmental conditions of man (44).

At least five categories of 'valuations' have been identified that are of major relevance for social work: Those pertaining to: human nature, man's relationship to other men in society, society in relation to man, the process of knowing, and the process of helping (mutaul aid). Under each category a series of values can be subsumed on a high level of abstraction, which in turn must be operationalized in crucible of practice.

To illustrate with selective examples:

28

1. Human Nature:	Man has inherent dignity and worth; Man is knowledgeable; Man can grow, change and develop throughout his entire lifetime;
2. Man's Relationship to Other Men:	Man has a right to self-determination among a series of choices available to him in society; Man has an obligation to be concerned with the welfare of his fellow men;
3. Society in Relation To Men:	Society has a right to expect people to participate in its affairs to enhance the common good; Society has an obligation to enhance man's potential for growth and development;
4. Process of Knowing:	"Truth" should be sought out regardless where the search for it may lead; Systematic procedure through use of the scientific method to discover "truth" about man and society will yield knowledge about man and society;
5. Process of Helping: (Mutual Aid)	Helping others is desirable: being helped carries no stigma; Any person's need for help is to be respected without bias or prejudice;

Conflicting valuations and inconsistent beliefs abound in every society, and social work value commitments are faced with equal conflicts and inconsistencies.

Purpose or Goals: Three major purposes or goals of social work span the continuum from "treatment" to "development": curative-ameliorative, preventive, and promotional-enhancing. Under each category a number of goals can be subsumed:

1. Curative-ameliorative: (Treatment-orientation)

To assist individuals, families or other small groups in coping with their problems in social functioning (social role performance);

To assist social organizations, neighborhoods or communities in coping with their problems that are related to problems of their members or residents;

To rehabilitate people who are defective in their social functioning (social role performances);

2. Preventive: (Action-orientation)

To identify potential areas of problems and to strengthen existing "healthy" forces (primary prevention);

To detect early symptoms of problems and to intervene at this stage to halt their spread (secondary prevention);

To limit the manifestations of problems through anticipatory action and rehabilitation (tertiary prevention);

(problems can be found among: individuals, small groups, social organizations, neighborhoods and communities);

3. Promotional-enhancing (Developmental Orientation)

To meet needs and enhance the social functioning of individuals, families or other small groups, to move towards existential fulfillment and maximum self-realization through social participation;

To enhance the maximum potential of social organizations, neighborhoods and communities, to insure the existential fulfillment and maximum self-realization of people through social participation.

In the not too distant past the curative treatment-oriented goals were accepted as the major province of social work. Intra- and interpersonal tensions and stress conditions, role conflicts, deviant behavior, age-connected isolation of people have been traditional problem areas for social work intervention.

With the advent of public health awareness and raised public consciousness about social problems, social work in the USA and in many other countries has moved toward greater prevention orientation. This calls for attention to large-scale social problems and for commitment to action for dealing with such persistent problems as poverty, juvenile delinquency, drug dependency, alcoholism, etc. The "War on Poverty" in 1964 in the US, furthermore, has led to the conception and execution of community action programs which have had a marked influence upon social work thinking and practice ever since.

Commitment to the third goal, that of promoting and enhancing the quality of life of the people of a society, is of still more recent origin. In the past, interest in furthering this goal was mostly expressed in the fields of recreation and education—notably informal and adult education—rather than in the field of social work (45). The developmental orientation, which now has become increasingly a part of the goals and practice of social work, particularly in the developing countries of the world, seeks to create conditions for people that allow them to fulfill themselves optimally, to comprehend the world of today and tomorrow, to find their place in it and to participate constructively and actively in their society as part of a larger world order. Fundamentally this aspect of social work is learning (*Bildung*— "formation") oriented—it is the social-cultural part of the social work continuum.

The continuum notion avoids rigidity. To treat a person's problem today can lead to preventive action against the further spread of this problem tomorrow. This in turn can lead to further growth and development of this person's life and of others later on. To illustrate: an older widowed person who has retired from work and feels lonely and isolated can be helped to meet other older people, to engage in activities with them, to participate in the organization of a club program for older people in order to counteract the loneliness and interpersonal isolation of others as well. By doing so he and others may be able to discover new interests and learn new things and feel useful at the same time. He can inform himself and others of additional problems that beset older adults in his community and region (e.g. inadequate public transportation, inaccessible health care facilities), and can learn to become instrumental in finding measures to deal with similar problems, through organizing other people and groups in the community or region by making facilitative use of a social worker as a change-agent.

Sanctions: Social work, like any other activity, is not practiced in a vacuum. It is given societal sanctions that are expressed through a degree of legal authority which is extended to the social work practitioner to perform his tasks. The actual practice of social work, i.e., the implementation of its purposes, is carried out by a variety of service agencies or by non-agency affiliated, autonomous social workers. When society is viewed as dynamic and ever-changing, accommodating conflicting forces and claims, rather than as static and harmonious, preserving a status quo then sanctioned by society, it does not imply an "establishment orientation" of social work nor a commitment to "adjustment functions" to insure conformity of people to the predominant cultural norms and adaptation at any price to prevailing social structures. It rather implies that social work is a force for social integration of people. Such integration connotes help towards "personalization", i.e. enabling a person to develop his (her) own new set of responses to societal expectations which have commensurate effects upon the social and cultural milieu. Thus, 'social integration' also means adaptation of the environment to the needs of the individual person (46).

Since the mission of social work is by definition people-oriented, inevitable conflicts arise when societal imperatives clash with the needs, desires, aspirations and wishes of people. To accept this conflict as natural and inherent in the very existence of social work is a fundamental axiom of its practice.

Social work is sanctioned to be carried out in social welfare agencies under governmental, non-governmental (voluntary) auspices, in industry, in trade unions, and in communal organizations and total institutions and also by independent non-agency affiliated practitioners as private entrepreneurs. The settings and auspices vary considerably from country to country. Depending on the purpose and orientation of the program or service offered through such organizational or institutional networks, the "consumers" of such services are referred to as "clients" or "patients", usually those who receive curative-ameliorative type services, or as "members", "partners", "constituents", "citizens", usually those who are involved in action or development programs designed to enhance their own well-being or those of other groups and organizations.

The sanction component includes the following aspects of practice: Types of programs or services offered; organizational, personnel, financial and administrative structures through which the programs or services are offered; nature of program or service delivery to people (matching between needs of people and programs or services to meet these needs); provision for planning and the creation of improved or of new types of programs and services when needed.

Knowledge: Knowledge upon which social work practice is based is derived from a variety of sources commonly referred to as disciplines, such as psychology, biology, sociology , social psychology, psychiatry, anthropology, pedagogy, law, theology, etc. It is also derived from the accumulated practice wisdom (practice theory) that has emerged in the course of social work activities over the years. When we speak of "knowledge" we need to differentiate between that which is definitely known (empirically verified), that which is tentatively known (hypothetically stated), that which is assumed to be known, and that which is clearly as yet unknown. Social work practice is predicated upon knowledge in its varying states and applied by practitioners. If such application results in ready and efficient performance, we speak of such technical expertness as "skills".

The following five categories have been found to be the essential knowledge areas: Growth and Behavior of Man in Society, Behavior and Development of Society (social structures and cultures), Human and Social Problems, Human Potentials and Social Opportunities, Modes of Intervention and their Impact upon People and Society, Knowledge-Building and Testing.

The following selective examples are illustrative:

1) Growth and Behavior of Man in Society: ("normal" and varying or deviating)	Man is a bio-psycho-socio-cultural being; Bio-psycho-socio-cultural subsystems are interacting and man's growth in these progresses "orderly", from simple to complex;

Man in each of these four subsystems is confronted with particular "developmental" tasks: engagement in these may be more or less stressful. Maladaptation to stress may lead to disease, pathology or deviant behavior.

2) Behavior and Development of Society (Social systems in persistence and change):

The major functions of society as a social system;

Behavior of groups and organizations is a system-response to changing functions, tasks, and expectations;

Social processes create social structures and vice versa;

Social role is the link between the individual and changing social structures and cultures, as personality in social interaction;

3) Human and Social Needs and Social Problems; Human Potentials and Social Opportunities

Disease in each of the four subsystems are maladaptations to stress which are amenable to intervention;

Nature and derivation of human and social needs; causation, etiology, correlates, scope, incidence, prevalence of social problems;

Responses by society over time to human and social needs and to social problems;

The nature and derivation of human potential for learning and development;

The nature of social opportunities for people of all ages in families, small groups and communities;

Obstacles in the realization of social opportunities by people;

	Creation of social opportunities; the goals and nature of a welfare society;
4) Modes of Intervention and Their Impact Upon People and Society:	Types of interventions (societal and social policies, education, therapy, social work, etc.)
	Impact of such intervention upon the lives of people and upon social structures;
5) Knowledge-Building and Testing:	Nature of the knowledge-building and inquiry process in the natural and social sciences and in applied fields (such as social work);
	Approach to knowledge testing and inquiry in the natural, social sciences and in applied fields (such as social work).

A range of concepts and propositions that make up the knowledge base of social work, analogous to these selected illustrations for each of the five categories, needs to be developed: this requires continuous revisions and augmentation in the light of newly developing information and knowledge (46 a).

Intervention Repertoire: This component refers to the "action of the practitioner which is directed to some part of social system or process with the intention of inducing a change in it" (47). Intervention aims at making a difference in outcome in the course of events. It is guided by a constellation of values, purposes, and knowledge and is based upon legal or institutional sanctions. It is justified on the basis of "creative altruism", as social work, historically and declaratively, has shown regard for or devotion to the interests of others through service; creativity is a necessary condition for effective service to other people.

This component of social work practice has been labelled "methods", identified as *social casework, social groupwork,* and *community organization.* In the USA as well as in Canada the development of the three social work "methods" has been almost synonymous with the development of social work practice itself. Each of these methods had different historical roots and therefore had developed differently with differing emphasis and foci.

"Casework emerged early as a method in social practice. Recognizable professional concepts were discernible in the charity worker's individualization of the person and his need, in friendly visiting, and in the ideas of "not alms, but a friend" and helping people to help themselves. In conceptualizing these ways of helping and in outlining a systematic method of study and diagnosis in the classic *Social Diagnosis* (1917), Mary Richmond gave social work the distinctive processes and techniques of casework.

The primary sociological basis of Mary Richmond's formulations was later supplanted by an approach based on psychoanalytical psychology with an overwhelming emphasis on individual change and adaptation. Social work, as expressed in psychoanalytically oriented casework and in the need (as opposed to intellectual) basis of human behavior, tended to be seen as more scientific and more professional than social work which stressed environmental influences and rational factors.

Social reform and social change—i.e., efforts toward changing social institutions and social conditions for man—have never been absent from the concern of social work, and notable social workers who came to be identified as caseworkers—e.g., Gordon Hamilton, Charlotte Towle, Bertha Reynolds—never lost sight of this aspect of social work's goals and functions. A major impetus toward environmental change and social action activities, however, came from other strands of social work, particularly from social group work.

The roots of social group work lie in the pragamatic philosophy of John Dewey of "learning by doing" and its application in the field of education. Social group work is also closely associated with the social reform approach of the settlement movement. The use of group experience to further individual and social change was a fundamental tenet of the National Association for the Study of Group Work (Lieberman, 1938). The writings of Edward Lindeman and Grace Coyle and the insights and experiments of Kurt Lewin and his followers have provided a practice for many "group movements" of our day.

Community organization shares with casework a common ancestry in the charity organization movement and shares with group work many similarities in approach. Concern with utilizing group experiences on a neighborhood and community level to effect social change was common to both community organization and group work. While group work tended to concentrate on the utilization of small face-to-face groups, community organization turned to larger groupings and organizational units in a community and also focused on intergroup activities. Fund raising for social welfare agencies and coordination and planning of health and welfare services in a local community were among the first concerns of community organization in the days of the charity organization movement. The mobilization of human, economic and organizational resources to create viable neighborhoods and communities became a major focus and connections were made also with the broader field of community development (Schwartz, 1965). The views of Robert Lane, Wilber Newsletter and Murray Ross are some of those which contributed to the early formation of community organization theory and practice" (48).

Undoubtedly the contributions of each "method" to a more inclusive, encompassing approach are fundamental and will continue to be the basis for all social work interventive efforts. However, the idea of 'method' in social work seems to have become inextricably tied up with a whole mode of approach and for many social workers encompasses the relevant knowledge and values as well as techniques (49). "Interventive acts and techniques are means to an end and are only significant when the end is defined in terms of social work purposes and values and the situation is accurately understood through the use of social work knowledge. It is through the conscious action of the social worker, who selects what is relevant for the particular situation before him, that the appropriate knowledge and values become integrated with intervention" (50).

This type of thinking has opened what has been a closed, rather narrowly conceived and segmented practice orientation. It makes it possible now to rearrange the knowledge base and practice wisdom plus the attendant methodological skills from casework, groupwork and community organization into new interventive repertoires and therefore to widen and broaden their application. The ingredients of the "methods" can be used for the widened purposes of social work and they can be applied to the total purpose continuum: "treatment" when social functioning of people is impaired, "action" when problems are to be prevented that impinge upon the social functioning of people, and "development" when social functioning is to be enhanced to achieve maximum self-realization for responsible and creative social participation, the realization of the political and social dimensions of human existence. The following five dimensions encompass the intervention repertoire: Specific targets of intervention; specific goals for intervention (these are deduced from the more general purposes of social work); steps in the intervention process; activities of the intervener, i.e., social worker (these include modalities, methods and techniques); the roles of the intervener, i.e. social worker.

1) Specific Targets: (also called "systems")

They are divided into micro and macro units. Micro units refer to:
- individuals (children, adolescents, young adults, middle aged persons, older adults, aged persons)
- families and networks of kin
- face-to-face groups

Macro units refer to:
- social organizations, agencies, institutions
- neighborhoods in a community
- total communities
- regional areas

We tend to speak of "micro or macro level intervention" with commensurate consequences in the steps and activities undertaken by the intervener.

2) Specific Goals: (the result of pre-selection, assessment and judgement by people, by social work practitioners jointly with people, and/or by functionaries in social organizations)

treatment oriented:
    e.g. to counsel a family with interpersonal relationship problems

action oriented
    e.g. to make a group of older people aware of their pension rights

development oriented
    e.g. to conduct a family life education program for a group of citizens

38

3) Steps in the Intervention Process: (A systematic procedure pursued in interacting, spiral-like patterns in micro or macro systems)	treatment oriented: —exploration of problems —study of problems —diagnosis —treatment goal formulation —treatment plan —implementation of treatment plan —use of feedback —evaluation action oriented —exploration and identification of problems or problem situatio —data collection of problems or situation —assessment of problems or situation —plan of action-for-change formulation —implementation of action —use of feedback —evaluation development oriented —exploration of needs and aspirations —study of needs and aspirations —assessment of needs and aspirations —goal formulation $\Big\}=$ defining —task specification $\quad$ objectives —provision of learning and living experiences —use of feedback —evaluation of experiences
4) Activities of the Intervener: (the "how" of intervention in micro or macro systems)	A series of modalities are available su‹ as interviews, group sessions and mee› ings, and conferences.

Incorporated in the use of interventive activities of the social worker are such techniques as: psychological support, information-giving, interpretation, clarification, development of insights, creation and use of groups and organizational structures, use of program media and tools, mobilization use and management of available human, material and technical resources, counselling, teaching, etc.

5) The Roles of the Intervener:

There are three *major* roles which the social worker performs:
1) enabler
2) broker
3) advocate

As an "enabler" he makes it possible for individuals or groups to help themselves, to utilize their motivation, capacities and strengths to optimum advantage. As a "broker" he negotiates and provides a liaison between social institutions, organizations, agencies and people in need of services of any kind (social, health, consumer, legal, etc.) As an "advocate" the social worker speaks up for the rights of people and groups and negotiates their access to services; at the same time he assists people in speaking up for themselves to demand quality programs and services to which they are entitled as a social benefit.

These three major roles are performed in judicious interplay; at times one role receives greater emphasis than another; in a particular situation a social worker (e.g. in an adult education enterprise) may want to stress the enabling role, while in another situation (e.g. as a guidance counselor) he may assume the broker role. In a community action program the social worker may perform the role of an advocate and also act as an enabler to the action group itself (51).

SOCIAL WORK INTERVENTION CHART

Target	Primary Goal Orientation		
	Treatment	Action	Development
Micro-Systems; Individual	Therapeutic Steps and Activities; Problem-Solving Steps and Activities		Need-Meeting and Enhancing Steps and Activities
Family Face-to-Face (small group)	Therapeutic Steps and Activities; Problem-Solving Steps and Activities	Problem-Solving Steps and Activities	Need-Meeting and Enhancing Steps and Activities
	Roles of: Enabler–Broker–Advocate		

Macro-Systems:
  Large Grouping
  Organization
  Neighborhood
  Community
		Problem-Solving Steps and Activities	Need-Meeting and Enhancing Steps and Activities

	Roles of: Enabler–Broker–Advocate		

Intervention on the macro-level of larger regional units of state, province, or nation occurs through social, respectively societal policy. Links between social work and social (societal) policy interventions are to be in existence with respect to all macro-systems through the deployment of social workers in social and societal policy formulation and planning tasks, among other involvements.

41

Supervision, Consultation and Administration

As an aid to increasing skill in performing these roles and activities and to providing direct mechanisms for review and self-control, social work practice utilizes *supervision* and consultation, while *administration* is perceived as a facilitative, indirect mechanism to make possible direct practice to people.

Supervision is a non-time-limited mandatory teaching/learning process which is geared to confront the practitioner (supervisee) singly or in groups with his (their) professional role, by a supervisor.
It aims to enable the social worker (supervisee) to achieve and to improve a capacity for systematic, goal oriented and significant interventive action, a capacity to evaluate and reflect such action in a disciplined way, and to gain a perspective relative to such action as a means of self-control (52).

Consultation involves a time-limited voluntary contractual relationship between an expert and a less-knowledgeable practitioner (consultee). It aims to strengthen the consultee in his designated role functioning by increasing his knowledge and skills to enhance his performance and is usually focused on a segment rather than on the totality of his work (53).

Administration of programs and services in social work has been defined as an *indirect facilitative* method of practice "which is concerned primarily with these activities: 1) translation of societal mandates into operational policies and goals to guide organizational behavior 2) designs of organizational structures and processes through which the goals can be achieved 3) securing of resources in the form of materials, staff, clients, and societal legitimation necessary for goal attainment and organizational continuity 4) selection and engineering of the necessary technologies 5) optimizing organizational behavior directed toward increased effectiveness and efficienc and 6) evaluation of organizational performance to facilitate systematic and continuous problem-solving" (53A). These activities go on at three levels in social welfare organizations: 1) institutional level 2) managerial level 3) technical level.

Major Approaches of the Social Work 'Methods'

As mentioned once before, the interventive stances in social work derive from and are still largely based on the practice wisdom and conceptual development of the three major "methods". While there are many attempts to re-conceptualize and re-cast these into multi-dimensional intervention stances (54), these attempts have not yet yielded a "generalist method". There is agreement that there are common features in the approaches of intervention on the micro level and common features on the macro level and that a division along those lines is more desirable than on an individual group-community dimension. (Social casework and social group work at present correspond roughly to intervention on the micro level and community organization and social planning on the macro level).

The three traditional "methods" have produced a series of different major approaches which serve as departure points for model-building of an intentive repertoire of social work. In summary they are as follows:

In Social Casework:

The Functional Approach is characterized by seeing the center for change as residing in the client (not in the worker); viewing casework as a method for administering some specific social service through an agency which gives the service focus, direction and content, and approaching the worker-client relationship as a process with an avowed lack of knowledge of how it will turn out. The worker's responsibility is for control of his part in the helping process, not for the achievement of any pre-determined end (55).

The Problem-Solving Approach holds that all human living is a problem-solving process and that a person's inability to cope with a

44

problem on his own is due to some lack of motivation, capacity or opportunity to work on, solve, or mitigate the problem in appropriate ways. Therefore, the activities of the social worker are aimed to: release, energize and give direction to a person's motivation and capacity for coping with the problems and to find and make accessible to the person opportunities and resources necessary to mitigation or solution of the problem (56).

The Psycho-Social Approach has embraced intervention in the situation on behalf of the client by a social worker and direct work with the individual (or several individuals). Treatment is individualized in terms of the worker's diagnostic understanding of the person-in-situation problem and is often referred to as 'environmental manipulation' on the one hand and 'insight therapy' on the other. Basic to all treatment is a therapeutically sound relationship that consists of a series of verbal and non-verbal communications between client and worker (57).

All three major approaches, although emphasizing certain aspects more pointedly, have a great deal in common, notably a dynamic and constant content: "the 4 p's: a *p*erson beset by a *p*roblem seeks some solution from a *p*lace; he is offered help by a social worker whose *p*rocess simultaneously engages and enhances his own powers and/or supplements his own resources through those in the community."

In Social Groupwork:

The Social Goals Approach assumes there is unity between social action and individual psychological health and views every group as possessing a potential for affecting social change. It looks at the worker as an influence person responsible for cultivation of social consciousness in groups, thus inculcating a value system. The social worker serves as a role model for people, stimulating and reinforcing modes of conduct appropriate to citizenship responsibility directed toward social change. The three basic areas of operation of the social worker are: the group goal-achieving processes, the members and workers interpersonal relations and individual self-actualization. The worker's activities are directed towards task accomplishment of the group that should lead to existential fulfillment of its members (58).

The Rehabilitation (remedial) Approach stresses that the group is a tool or context for 'treatment' of the individual. Toward this end it establishes diagnostic goals for each individual by the social worker and the group program is primarily evaluated for its therapeutic potential rather than for its creative and expressive qualities. The worker uses a problem-solving approach to achieve his treatment goals for each group member through direct means of influence (as object of identification, as motivator-stimulator, as symbol of values and norms, as executive) and indirect means of influence (use of group structures and group processes) as well as through extra-group means (persons or institutions in the client's social environment (59).

The Interactional (reciprocal) Approach pre-supposes an organic, systemic relationship between the individual and society and the small group is the field in which individual and societal functioning can be nourished. Here the group is in a position of preeminence and emphasis is placed on engagement of the members in the process of interpersonal relations. It is from this state of involvement that members may call upon each other in their own or common cause. The interactionist emphasizes experience and affect, step-by-step process and situational, rather than structural, description of people in difficulty. The social worker here is a mediator and carries out a number of tasks such as searching out the common ground between the group member's perception of his own need and the social demand upon him, detecting and challenging obstacles which obscure the common ground contributing data and lending a vision, as well as defining requirements between members and workers (60).

The developmental approach is equally process-oriented but views the group primarily as an "arena of training", preparing the members for a transfer of their experiences to other types of life experiences. Therefore, it is more educationally and learning focused and places emphasis upon the development of people and groups over time. It postulates that the social worker fashions his skills from the demands of five major phases of group life: 1) approach-avoidance 2) power and control 3) intimacy 4) differentiation 5) termination Setting a contract specifying the rights and obligations of group members, agency and worker is at the root of purposeful relationships that constitute the means for task accomplishment directed towards learning, action or personality growth (61).

In all four approaches the use of interpersonal relationships in face-to-face groups and the deployment of various roles by the social worker to engage members in common efforts of problem-solving are clearly evident. The development and action-oriented stance is quite pronounced, although the remedial model shows many tangential touches with the more treatment-focused approaches of social casework.

In Community Organization:

Problem-solving is an underlying theme of the approaches of community organization as well. In the recent literature three models have been elaborated: 1) locality (community) development 2) social action and 3) social planning (62).

Community development emphasizes the broad association of people at the local neighborhood-community level in goal formulation and action to create conditions of economic and social progress for a whole community. *Social action* is oriented to bring about major structural and cultural changes in organizations, institutions or agencies through organizing a segment of a population to obtain a more equitable share of the resource-pie in the larger community or nation. *Social planning* stresses a rational, technical process of solving substantive social problems, such as delinquency, poor housing, mental illness, etc., with a concern for establishing and delivering goods and services to people.

The various purposes of these different approaches in community organization are the results of diverse purposes of groups, organizations and movements which are engaged in community organizational efforts.

In another scheme it is suggested that, although community organization and social planning are aspects of a whole, practice is carried on with somewhat different emphasis and methods in three organizational contexts: 1) promotion of voluntary associations 2) program development in direct health and social service agencies 3) problem-solving on an interorganizational basis in community planning and resource-allocating organizations (63).

Distinctive to all these approaches is the fact that the outcome sought is not increased power for a particular group, nor necessarily a closer integration of a community (although this may occur), but changes in the policies, priorities, programs and services of organizations whose activities directly affect the people who have a common problem.

Community development approaches have many features in common with those in social casework and social groupwork. In all three the overall focus is for people to acquire problem-solving skills although individuals in trouble need help in solving their problems differently than members of a community group that wants to organize to obtain better housing facilities. In each situation the social worker has to explore, study and diagnose (assess) the situation, the conditions and the people involved and based on his diagnosis (assessment) he attempts to formulate a plan and a structure for treatment, action, or task implementation (whatever the case may be) together with the people or groups involved, to carry out the plans and to evaluate the outcome. The involvement of people all along the way is an indispensable ingredient; they must achieve mastery over their fate. Intervention, therefore, is never unilateral; it is always bilateral and mutual.

There are also differences: Social casework and groupwork approaches by their very nature concentrate on smaller units as targets (individuals, families, face-to-face groups) and therefore are microcosmic oriented, while community organization models with their concern for larger social units are macrocosmic in intent and design and therefore become closer related to social and societal policy and their strategies and methods. Here is a bridge between social work, social and societal policy, a major tangential point in the total intervention mechanisms.

Treatment-focused intervention—whether for individuals, families, small groups—represents one aspect of the continuum of social work practice. It can be and often is practiced in many settings such as child guidance centers, family service agencies, housing units, hospitals, clinics, schools, mental health centers, industry, labor unions, in fact wherever curative intervention is indicated.

Action-focused intervention usually involves small groups, organization, neighborhoods; it represents another aspect of the social work continuum. Its practice takes place in many instances in the same types of settings as mentioned, provided the purpose of the intervention is "action" rather than "cure". In addition, it occurs in community, development bodies, action agencies, churches, etc.

Development-focused intervention also can take place in the settings described. However, the bulk of this type of program is offered more often in youth development centers, group service

48

agencies, total institutions, settlement houses, adult education institutions and organizations.

Increasingly, there are multi-purpose centers in operation which combine many programs and services under one roof, under one or several auspices in order to maximize accessibility and availability of services to clients and consumers.

The efforts to conceptualize various approaches to social work intervention, to build models is of recent origin and in all likelihood will continue. In addition, sporadic research attempts, notably in North America and some countries of Western Europe, have been undertaken to subject social work practice to systematic scrutinizing and to convert tentative knowledge into more definitive knowledge, since the most fundamental task of a profession is to build its body of knowledge so that its methods of intervention may prove increasingly effective in achieving the results to which its practice is directed. By this criterion, social work practice in all types of intervention everywhere is still in a rudimentary state of development, although there are differences of degree, e.g. casework intervention has a more highly developed knowledge base than social groupwork which in turn is less rudimentary than community work intervention.

Education for Social Work

"Stated in broad terms the purpose of social work education is to prepare personnel for the performance of social welfare functions in a variety of social institutions, particularly in the fields of health, education, welfare and the judicial system. Generally, social welfare personnel can be categorized as follows:

1) policy, planning and administration personnel
2) supervisory and consultative personnel
3) teachers, trainers and researchers
4) direct service practitioners
5) technical and auxiliary personnel. (64)"

The comparative study of *National Social Service Systems* (65) h shown that in many countries all over the world educational institutions for the preparation of social workers have been established by now, although no overall strategy for social welfare manpower has evolved in any of the countries studied.

A *separate monograph,* to be published, will discuss designs of social work education in some detail, specifying objectives, levels, curriculum content, methodology and organization and reviewing trends, problems and issues for today and tomorrow.

REFERENCES

1) UNITED NATIONS, Economic and Social Council, *Reappraisal of the United Nations, Social Service Programme,* New York, 1965.
   UNITED NATIONS, Department of Economic and Social Affairs, *Training for Social Work; Third International Survey,* New York, 1958.
   National Social Service Systems, A comparative Study, U.S. Department of Health, Education and Welfare, Division of International Activities, Washington, D.C., September 1970.
   This definition has been adopted by the Board of Directors of the National Association of Social Workers (NASW) in the United States as part of its Model Statutes for the legal regulation of social work: (1970)
   "Social work is a professional activity of helping individuals, groups or communities enhance or restore their capacity for social functioning and create societal conditions favorable to this goal."
   The Katholische Fachhochschule in Nordrhein-Westfalen (W. Germany) has agreed upon the following descriptive definition in 1970:
   "Sozialarbeit ist gerichtet auf die Entwicklung und Foerderung sozialer Prozesse, um Faehigkeiten eigenstaendigen sozialen Verhaltens zu entfalten, konstruktive Loesungen von Konfliktsituationen zu ermoeglichen, und sozial Defizite in der Gesellschaft auszugleichen."
2) HELGE PETERS, *Die Misslungene Professionalisierung der Sozialarbeit* in "Sozialarbeit als Beruf", Juventa Verlag, Muenchen, 1971 S.99-123.
3) AMITAI ETZIONI, *The Semi-Professions and Their Organization,* The Free Press, New York, 1969.

51

4) EVERETT C. HUGHES, *Men and Their Work.*
The Free Press, Glencoe, Ill. 1958.
5) DONALD FELDSTEIN, "Do We Need Professions in Our
Society" in *Social Work,* Vol. 16, No. 4, October 1971, Nat:
Association of Social Workers, New York.
KURT REICHERT, "Professionalisierung der Sozialarbeit in
den Vereinigten Staaten" in *Sozialarbeit als Beruf,* op. cit.
6) *National Social Service Systems,* op. cit.
7) "Working Definition of Social Work Practice" prepared by Commission on Social Work Practice of the National Association of
Social Workers in 1956 and revised by William E. Gordon in
1962 and Louis Lowy in 1965.
8) HARRIET M. BARTLETT, *The Common Base of Social Work
Practice.* National Association of Social Workers, New York,
1970.
9) HAROLD L. WILENSKY and CHARLES N. LEBEAUX,
Industrial Society and Social Welfare, Russell Sage Foundation,
New York, 1958, p. 342. (A second, revised edition is available
in paperback through The Free Press, New York, 1966)
10) Adapted from the works of: Talcott Parsons, *The Social System,*
Free Press, Glencoe, Ill., 1951, Kingsley Davis, *Human Society,*
Macmillan Co., New York, 1949, Roland L. Warren, *The Com-
munity in America,* Rand McNally, Chicago, 1963.
11) "The Triple Revolution", Ad-Hoc Committee, Santa Barbara,
California, 1964. Robert Theobald, *Free Men and Free Markets.*
Doubleday & Co., Garden City, N.Y. 1963.
12) See: Reports issued by United Nations, op. cit. Anton Hunziker,
*Kantonales Recht im Wandel: Vom Fuersorgerecht zum
Sozialhilferecht,* Antonius Verlag, Solothurn, 1971.
12 a) U.S. DEPARTMENT OF HEALTH, EDUCATION, AND
WELFARE, Social Security Administration, "Social Security
Programs Throughout the World: 1973".
13) World Health Organization Definition of "Health": It is a
"state of complete physical, mental and social well-being."
14) ALFRED KAHN, *Issues in American Social Work,* "The Function of Social Work in the Modern World", Columbia University
Press, New York, 1959.
15) REUBEN HILL, *Family Development Over Three Generations,*
Harvard University Press, Cambridge, Mass., 1970.

16) JOHN GALBRAITH: *The New Industrial State*, Harvard University Press, Cambridge, Mass., 1967.
Private Wants and Public Needs, ed. E.W. Phelps, W.W. Norton Co., New York, 1962.
17) BARBARA WARD, "The Responsibility of Power", *Nationalism and Ideology*, W.W. Norton & Co., 1966.
18) "The War on Poverty". Programs in the United States have enunciated this principle, originally written into the "Economic Opportunity Act of 1964".
19) ROGER DANIELS and HARRY H.L. KITANO, *American Racism: Exploration of the Nature of Prejudice*, Prentice Hall, Inc., Englewood Cliffs, New Jersey, 1970.
20) WILENSKY and LEBEAUX, op. cit., p. 341-348.
21) JOHN HORTON, "Order and Conflict Theories of Social Problems", *Radical Perspectives on Social Problems*, ed. Lindenfeld, also in: *American Journal of Sociology*, May 1966, pp. 701-713.
22) ABRAHAM MASLOW, *Motivation and Personality*, W.B. Saunders Co., New York, 1954.
23) ERIK H. ERIKSON, *Childhood and Society*, W.W. Norton & Co., New York, 1950. "Identity and the Life Cycle", *Papers by Erik H. Erikson*, International Universities Press, New York, 1959.
24) ANTON HUNZIKER, op. cit., p. 12.
25) ALVIN L. SCHORR and EDWARD C. BAUMHEIER, "Social Policy", *Encyclopedia of Social Work*, National Association of Social Workers, New York, 1971, p. 1362.
26) Ibid.
27) Ibid.
28) *United Nations Reports*, op. cit. *1970 Report on the World Social Situation*, Social Development Division of the Dept. of Economic and Social Affairs, United Nations, New York.
29) T.H. MARSHALL, *Social Policy in the Twentieth Century*, 2nd. Edition, London, Hutchinson & Co., 1967.
30) "The Changing Role of Social Welfare" in *National Social Service Systems*, op. cit., Chap. II, p. 3-6.
31) ANTON HUNZIKER, op. cit., p. 9.
32) ALVIN SCHORR and EDW. BAUMHEIER, op. cit. p. 1370.
33) T. STUDER: "Wandlungen des menschlichen Zusammenlebens in unserer Zeit, Folgerungen fuer die Sozialarbeit der Zukunft" Schweiz. Berufsverband der Sozialarbeiter, Bern, 1969.

34) *Toward the Year 2000,* Harvard University Commission, in *Daedalus,* 1969, Cambridge, Mass.
35) ROBERT PERLMAN, "Social Planning and Community Organiztion: Approaches", *Encyclopedia of Social Work,* 1970, p. 1338
36) Ibid.
37) ALFRED J. KAHN, *Theory and Practice of Social Planning,* Russell Sage Foundation, New York, 1969.
ROBERT MORRIS and ROBERT BINSTOCK, *Feasible Planning For Social Change,* Columbia University Press, New York, 1966.
38) GORDON W. ALLPORT, *Personality, A Psychological Interprettion,* Holt Co., New York, 1937.
39) WERNER BOEHM, *Curriculum Study* of the Council on Social Work Education, 1959, Volume I, New York.
40) HARRIETT M. BARTLETT, op. cit.
41) ANTON HUNZIKER, op. cit.
42) "Working Definition of Social Work Practice", as amended in Harriet M. Bartlett, op. cit., pp. 51-61.
43) GUNNAR MYRDAL at the 15th International Conference of Social Welfare, Helsinki, 1968.
44) J.M. BOCHENSKI, "Der Wert" in *Wege zum Philosophischen Denken,* Herder Buecherei, Freiburg i. Br., 1959.
45) LOUIS LOWY, *Adult Education and Group Work,* Whiteside-Morrow, New York, 1955. LOUIS LOWY, *Neue Wege in der Erwachsenenbildung* Haus Der Kathol, Frauen. Duesseldorf, 196
46) ANTON HUNZIKER, op. cit., p. 12.
46 a) LOUIS LOWY, LEONARD BLOKSBERG, HERBERT T. WALBERG, *Teaching Records,* Council on Social Work Education, New York, 1973. Part I, An attempt at development of conceptual matrices.
47) HARRIETT M. BARTLETT, op. cit., p. 161.
48) LOUIS LOWY, LEONARD BLOKSBERG, and HERBERT T. WALBERG, *Integrative Learning and Teaching in Schools of Social Work,* Association Press, New York, 1971, pp. 30-32.
49) HARRIETT M. BARTLETT, op. cit., p. 164.
50) Ibid.
51) This type of thinking and conceptualization has been elaborated in the North American social work literature since the late sixties See also publications by the National Association of Social Workers, Council on Social Work Education in New York,

syllabi of schools of social work in the United States and Canada.

2) LOUIS LOWY, "Definition of Supervision", mimeographed, 1970.
3) LYDIA RAPOPORT, "Consultation on Social Work", *Encyclopedia,* op. cit.
3 a) ROSEMARY S. SARRI, *Encyclopedia of Social Work,* 1972, p. 47.
4) The Council on Social Work Education has sponsored several workshops and many schools of social work are engaged in experimentations to offer multi-method courses or to develop courses in "social work practice", at least during the first year of the two-year graduate program. During the second year the trend is towards concentrating on one level of intervention (micro or macro) which frequently corresponds to casework/groupwork (micro level) and community work and social planning (macro level).
5) RUTH E. SMALLEY, *Theory for Social Work Practice,* Columbia University Press, New York, 1967.
6) HELEN HARRIS PERLMAN, *Social Casework: A Problem-Solving Process,* University of Chicago, Chicago, 1967.
7) FLORENCE HOLLIS, *Casework: A Psychosocial Therapy,* Random House, New York, 1964.
8) GRACE L. COYLE, *Group Work with American Youth,* Harper and Bros., New York, 1948.
9) ROBERT VINTER (ed.), *Readings in Group Work Practice,* Campus Publishers, Ann Arbor, Michigan, 1968.
0) WILLIAM SCHWARTZ and SERAPIO ZALBA (eds.), *The Practice of Group Work,* Columbia University Press, New York, 1971.
1) SAUL BERNSTEIN and LOUIS LOWY (eds.), *Untersuchungen zur Sozialen Gruppen-Arbeit,* Lambertus Verlag, Freiburg, i. B., 1969.
2) JACK ROTHMAN, "Three Models of Community Organization Practice", *Social Work Practice,* Columbia University Press, 1968, New York.
3) ARNOLD GURIN et al, *Community Organization Curriculum in Graduate Social Work Education,* Council on Social Work Education, New York, 1970.
4) WERNER BOEHM, "Education for Social Work", *Encyclopedia,* op. cit., p. 257.
5) *National Social Service Systems,* op. cit., Chapter V.